Why Do Things Fall?

If...Then

Rory McCallum

COMPUTER SCIENCE For the REAL World™

Rosen Classroom™

Have you ever dropped an object? Do objects fall or float in the air? Let's find out by testing different things!

Unless the object is a balloon, it will probably fall. That's because of gravity. On Earth, gravity pulls objects to the ground.

The rule of gravity says: "If you let go of something, then it will fall." Let's test objects that are heavy and light.

Bricks are heavy. Will a brick fall if you let go of it? Yes. If you let go of a brick, then it will fall.

Feathers are light. Will a feather fall if you let go of it? Yes. If you let go of a feather, then it will fall.

Let's think of objects that are big and small. Cars are big. Will a car fall if you let go of it? Yes. If you let go of a car, then it will fall.

Coins are small. Will a coin fall if you let go of it? Yes. If you let go of a coin, then it will fall.

Let's test objects that are thin or round. Paper is thin. Will paper fall if you let go of it? Yes. If you let go of paper, then it will fall.

A basketball is round. Will a basketball fall if you let go of it? Yes. If you let go of a basketball, then it will fall.

All objects fall on Earth. You can learn about gravity by testing any object you find. Make sure not to break anything!

Words to Know

basketball

brick

car

feather